HISTORIC HOMES *of* JEFFERSON, TEXAS

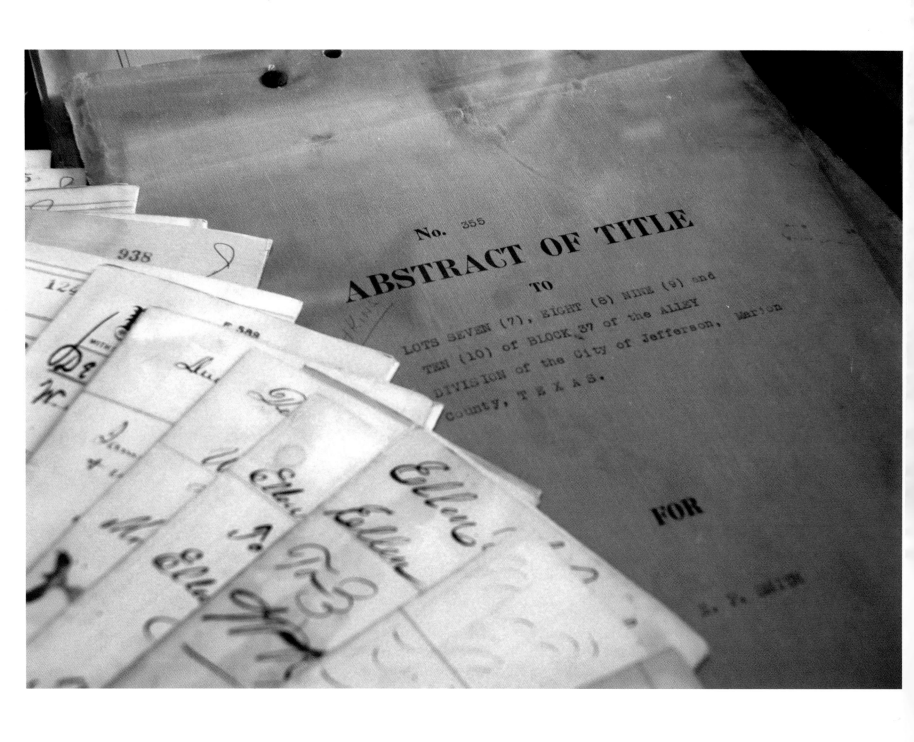

No. 355

ABSTRACT OF TITLE

TO

LOTS SEVEN (7), EIGHT (8) NINE (9) and
TEN (10) of BLOCK 37 of the ALLEY
DIVISION of the City of Jefferson, Marion
County, T E X A S.

FOR

HISTORIC HOMES *of* JEFFERSON, TEXAS

CHERYL MACLENNAN

December 2017

Enjoy your stay at The Magnolias.
Please come back and visit us again!

Sincerely,

Kim & Steve Shaw

PELICAN PUBLISHING COMPANY
GRETNA 2011

*The word "Pelican" and the depiction of a pelican
are trademarks of Pelican Publishing Company, Inc.,
and are registered in the U.S. Patent and Trademark Office.*

Library of Congress Cataloging-in-Publication Data

MacLennan, Cheryl.
  Historic homes of Jefferson, Texas / Cheryl MacLennan.
      p. cm.
  Includes bibliographical references.
      ISBN 978-1-4556-1484-4 (hardcover : alk. paper) — ISBN 978-1-4556-1485-1 (e-book) 1.
Architecture, Domestic—Texas— Jefferson—History—19th century. 2. Public architecture—Texas—
Jefferson—History—19th century. 3. Jefferson (Tex.)—Buildings, structures, etc. 4. Jefferson (Tex.)—
History. I. Title.
  NA7238.J36M33 2011
  728'.3709764193—dc22
                              2011011993

Color photography produced by Cheryl MacLennan.

Black-and-white photography courtesy Historic American Building Survey, Library of Congress.

Map of Jefferson, Texas, is from the 1871 Bird's Eye View map series, by Herman Brosius, courtesy of Amon Carter Museum, Fort Worth, Texas.

Printed in China
Published by Pelican Publishing Company, Inc.
1000 Burmaster Street, Gretna, Louisiana 70053

To Fred McKenzie and Cecilia Newton

1872

BIRD'S EYE VIEW OF

JEFFERSON

TEXAS.

Drawn by H. Brosius

REFERENCES:

Contents

Preface

My interest in and fondness for the East Texas town of Jefferson began more than twenty-five years ago, during a weekend stay at the historic Excelsior Hotel. I was entranced by the town's old Southern charm. It seemed that time had stood still. I imagined horses and buggies traveling up and down the brick streets. Since my first visit, Jefferson's population has remained essentially the same. The town has two thousand residents and two traffic lights.

Fortunately for us today, Jefferson was spared the modern city developers' attitude of "tear it down and build it new." In the 1970s, there were only a handful of bed and breakfasts and just a few homes in restoration. Today, as I visit and photograph these wonderful houses, I find most have been restored to their original splendor. Many are private residences, weekend getaways, or B&Bs.

After attending the Annual Candlelight Christmas Home Tour a couple of years ago, I wanted to learn more about the family history and detail of each house. With my passion for history, architecture, and uncovering the essence of a forgotten time, I began to photographically document many of Jefferson's historic structures.

I began to uncover the details with help from local historic organizations, the Jessie Allen Wise Garden Club, museum archives, and Fred McKenzie and other residents. I soon learned there were more than 135 historic-certified sites, buildings, and homes in Jefferson (second only to Galveston in Texas). This book highlights twenty-five historic buildings and showcases some of the town's beautiful home interiors.

Fred McKenzie at Books on the Bayou was my beginning inspiration. He was always ready to share colorful stories of the houses and the families who occupied the town's historic homes. Fred's enthusiasm for storytelling was legendary, and I spent many a Saturday evening listening to the tales and legends he would recall. Fred grew up in the area and had personal relationships with many local families. His ninety years of living and writing in Jefferson made him an invaluable resource.

Many people have been generous about sharing their family histories and allowing me to photograph their homes inside and out. I believe it is important to know where we come from and to honor the past. I hope you will enjoy this photo-remembrance of a historic town and its homes along the banks of the Big Cypress Bayou.

Early Architecture

Early Texas Architecture

Three primary criteria—geography, availability of materials, and cultural backgrounds of the builders—determined the character of early buildings in Texas. Anglo-Americans and African Americans first settled East Texas, and both groups came from the southern United States.

After the Louisiana Purchase, it was easiest for migrants to travel over land from Louisiana to Texas. Many settlers floated down the Mississippi River to the Red River and then traveled up the Red River into Texas.

After the Texas Revolution in 1836, land grants opened up the area for migration. The majority of the people came from the southern states, but some came all the way from the East Coast. These new landowners brought popular building styles from their former areas. Greek Revival was made popular by Thomas Jefferson as a vernacular style of the 1820s, and it was highly used until after the Civil War.

Greek Revival Architecture

The Greek style combined simple elegance with a sense of grandeur, using building materials available in the remote new frontier of East Texas.

Inspired by Greece, the oldest democracy in the world, Greek Revival has been used in Washington, D.C., for many of the federal buildings. It became widely popular throughout the South. Often simple white clapboard was the siding, and dark green was the choice for the trim and window shutters. Folklore explains that red was used for the doors of homes to welcome visitors or people passing through. The color alerted travelers that the owners would allow visitors a place to stop and rest or perhaps board for the night.

Columns or pillars are fundamental features of a Greek Revival home, sending a message of grandeur and strength. Symmetry is a central theme, which the Southern builders accentuated with wide, airy porches.

Most of the historic homes in the Jefferson area were made from materials native to the area. Long leaf pine was used for floors, exterior bricks were made by hand from the red clay soil, and cypress wood was made into wallboards and shingles. Slaves who came with the new landowners produced many of the construction materials, such as hand-forged hinges, hardware, and bricks. Their talents greatly contributed to the creation of the finely built homes.

Several of the homes in the Jefferson area followed another vernacular style known as the French Louisiana raised cottage, which was popular throughout the region at the time. Their design had raised piers and stairs leading to the main house level, leaving an open area underneath, usually covered with latticework. That area was commonly used for cart or buggy storage. Jefferson's proximity to the Big Cypress Bayou, combined with the moist Gulf of Mexico winds, made the raised cottages the perfect dwellings for people living in or near the flood plains.

Boom Years of Jefferson

Nestled in the northeast corner of Texas near the Louisiana border, Jefferson sits along a bend in the Big Cypress Bayou. The navigable bayou that established Jefferson as a far-inland port was the result of a natural dam in the Red River known as the "Great Raft."

The area's earliest inhabitants were the Caddo Indians who resided along the banks of Caddo Lake. In the 1830s, settlers began to arrive in the first of three waves of colonization. A man named Allan Urquhart offered settlers land in his claim on Cypress Bayou, and many moved to what is now Jefferson. He began a ferry across Cypress Bayou at the end of present-day Houston Street.

Urquhart, a surveyor for the Republic of Texas, laid out his land parcel at right angles to Cypress Bayou. Around the same time, another entrepreneur, Daniel Alley, obtained 586 acres adjoining Urquhart's land. Alley plotted his streets differently from Urquhart, aligning them according to the points on a compass. The plats are divided at Line Street and can be viewed today in an obvious division of the two sections of the city. Urquhart did not live in Jefferson, whereas Alley became a pillar in the community and, soon after establishing his development, deeded an entire block to house the courthouse and jail.

Next, pioneers from 1846 to the Civil War put down roots in Jefferson. Finally, after the Civil War, many people settled in Jefferson looking for a fresh start in the great immigration wave of the 1870s. Countless family histories record coming by steamer to Jefferson and then traveling by land to their new homes.

In 1872, the census for Jefferson reported a population of 7,297, composed of all classes and professions. Many of the inhabitants had arrived from New Orleans, bringing with them their elaborate furniture, fashions, and ideas. For a number of years, Jefferson served as the primary shipping point for cotton and was one of the largest mercantile cities in the state. The port was second only to Galveston in the amount of freight and passengers coming to Jefferson.

By 1873, two major events threatened the future of the bustling river port. The first was the building of the Texas and Pacific Railroad, which bypassed Jefferson. The second event was the destruction of the Great Red River Raft, composed of fallen trees, intertwined roots, collected silt, grasses, moss, and vines. With the invention of nitroglycerin, the United States Corps of Engineers blasted away the natural barrier. This destruction caused the water to disperse downstream and the depth of the Big Cypress Bayou to drop to a point where the steamboats could no longer reach the city of Jefferson. As a result, the population declined. After forty years of intense activity, time essentially stopped by 1880.

Although a smaller city now, Jefferson has continued to flourish. Many descendants of early settlers still call Jefferson home. Today this town of two thousand has one of the state's largest collections of residences dating from the late 1800s, with more than 135 state and nationally recognized historic structures.

Homes from 1850-1860

Rogers–Presbyterian Manse

211 Delta at Alley Street

Considered the oldest home in Jefferson, the Manse is one of the finest examples of Greek Revival architecture. The early structure faced Alley Street and was built by Charles G. Peel as his family residence. It was a one-story frame house covered by clapboard, elevated above ground level on a brick foundation. It was said to have consisted of two rooms.

The second construction occurred in 1850 extending the home to its full size. The home was located in a residential area; however, it was situated on a corner of a main route to the wharfs in town. To prevent the mule-run carts from turning too soon across the property, an iron post with a wheel from a gear mechanism off a ship was placed on the corner. It served as a pulley for heavy loads being transported to the loading docks.

In 1856, the property was sold to Gen. James Harrison Rogers, a prominent lawyer in Jefferson. Rogers made his home law library available to East Texas lawyers and students. The house was acquired by the Cumberland Presbyterian Church in 1903 for use as their manse (home for the church pastor), and it served in that capacity for fifty years.

In 1957, the property was purchased and restored by the Jessie Allen Wise Garden Club and used for club meetings and as a historic showcase museum on annual Historic Home Pilgrimages. The home changed hands again in the 1960s, purchased by Martin Jurow, producer of *Breakfast at Tiffany's* and the *Pink Panther* series. The Manse became his family's vacation home.

The structure's plan is a simple rectangle with a hip roof over the enclosed portion of the house and again over the two porticos. It features a central hallway with two double doors at either end for ventilation and two rooms on each side. Since the house sat on a corner, there are two tetra-style porticos on each entrance.

HABS 1936 photograph

The main entrance has fluted Doric columns, and the opposite west side has square columns with molded capitols. Another typical period feature is the double front door with sidelights on both sides and a transom light above. This allows natural light into the home while the portico roof shades the glass from the strong summer sun. The Delta Street front door molding has very elaborate carvings and embellishment that shares the fine woodwork of the time.

The home has been since acquired by Capt. Laura Omer, United States Navy Nurse Corps (retired). Captain Omer has restored the home to the finest detail, and it is now her private residence.

Well-documented during the 1936 Historic American Building Survey (HABS), the home is documented in the Library of Congress. It is listed on the National Register of Historic Places and received the Texas Historical marker in 1966. This home also received recognition by the U.S. Department of Interior for its beauty and its worthiness of preservation.

East door detail

Manse central hallway

Sagamore

201 Dixon

The home now known as the Sagamore was built in 1852. It is not certain who built the home, but one of the early owners and perhaps its builder was Henry Scott, part owner of the first ice plant in Texas (historically marked at the eastern edge of Jefferson).

The home features a simple design in the vernacular Louisiana style. It was common in this era for local people to build homes similar to those in the New Orleans area.

The Sagamore started as a small two-room home constructed with wooden pegs. The basic style of many of the early homes had a great central hall creating a "dog trot." This was a practical architectural feature in hot climates in the years before air conditioning. The "dog trot" was designed to catch breezes and cool the rooms. The home's roofline is another interesting element, with the subtle change in the pitch of the roof above the front porch. Later owners painted the home bright red with white trim, which accentuated the Louisiana style.

The home got its name through a joke made about its faulty floor. According to local lore, early owners could not remedy the problem. When Hubert Scantlin and his family moved into the house in the 1940s, he vowed the floor would "sag no more." The home was repaired, but the nickname stuck.

The Sagamore was briefly owned by the Presbyterian Church before being sold to its current owners is 2003.

Blue Bonnet Farm

Highway 2208

The original portion of the home known as the Blue Bonnet Farm was built in 1847 on a rise close to Trammel's Trace, an old Indian and horse-trading trail that ran from Galveston to St. Louis. The home may have served as a way station for travelers to rest their horses and receive lodging.

The residence owes its heritage to two remarkable ladies. The first was Jane Fox Cutrer, a widow from Mississippi who married Hiram A. Cutrer of Jefferson and, after his death, oversaw construction of the single-level frame home they had envisioned. This home was completed in 1869. It is believed she then attached a two-room cabin (dating from 1847) to form a rear wing, or "ell."

The second singular influence on the home was Dolly Bell Key, who acquired it in 1937, restored it faithfully, and then adapted it to its surroundings in a manner that made it a "Louisiana raised cottage." She bricked in a lower level for the rear wing, added wrought iron railings for its galleries, and centered the enclosed, landscaped area with a fountain.

On the front of the home, the double doors with sidelights are typical of the time. The sidelights help illuminate the home and enable the homeowners to see people at the door. Along with regular locks, the front doors have wrought iron brackets that hold a board in place to block intruders.

After the home's restoration, Dolly Bell Key added period furniture and opened it to the public on September 22, 1940,

as Jefferson's first museum. She kept detailed records of each item on display. Several were Key family heirlooms, including a piano that had belonged to Dolly Bell's grandmother and had been shipped by steamboat from New Orleans to Jefferson.

Today the home is on a route into historic Jefferson and is still shaded by red elms probably planted by the Cutrer family.

The lure of Trammel's Trace remains. In 1966, the home received its Texas Historical Marker.

Current view of the enclosed bottom floor.

HABS 1936 photograph showing raised house.

Alley-Carlson

501 Walker

The house on Walker Street was built by Daniel Alley and is considered one of the oldest surviving homes in Texas. Alley is believed to have used the home as his in-town office when it was first built.

The first full-time occupants were Augustus Bosworthy, a steamboat captain and his brother Henry. In 1861, the house was given to Alley's son, Daniel Alley Jr., as a wedding present. Four generations of the family owned the home until 1991. Mrs. Mary Carlson, a granddaughter of the Alley family, returned home in 1932 to care for her mother. Her mother was affectionately known as "Miss Mary" and was remembered for her many years of community service in connection with the formation of the Jessie Allen Wise Garden Club.

After Miss Mary's death, her daughter continued to own the property until 1991 when she donated many of the original family furnishings and contents to the Jefferson Historical Society and Museum. This donation was made with the understanding that the house and its contents should continue to reflect the lifestyle of the antebellum period and the four generations who lived in the home.

The home's interior has many of the typical Greek Revival features: sixteen-foot ceilings in the central hallway with rooms off to the side, lined in cypress board. Also, the home was decorated with bead paneling, which was originally cut and milled on the Alley's plantation near Jefferson. Many of the family furnishings, which traveled with the Alley's in the1820s from Virginia, are still present. One prized piece is an original wooden steamer trunk used to ship Miss Mary's wedding gifts.

DeWare~Cavalier

202 E. Dixon

The home was built in the 1850s and originally served as a tavern for travelers passing through the area. Later it became the home for Dr. DeWare Sr.'s family.

The Cavalier family from Dallas purchased the home in 1980 and restored it to its present glory. It was used as a family retreat before becoming a bed and breakfast.

A local preservationist once remarked, "We aren't the owners of these wonderful historic homes; we are only the custodians for a time."

Door detail

A signature from an early resident.

Woods~French Townhouse

502 Walker

The French Townhouse, also known as the Woods home, is one of the most distinctive homes in Jefferson. Daniel Alley, the town's cofounder, built the home, which probably served as his first residence. Later the home became a wedding gift for Alley's daughter.

The property was sold in 1870 to Samson Eagan for $1,000. Perry M. Woods owned the house the longest and was its namesake.

In 1934, Pres. Franklin Roosevelt's team of historic architects traveled across America to identify and survey historic properties. The home was described as a French Gothic townhouse of the New Orleans trade era. The name, French Townhouse, stuck.

Different from most other Jefferson residences, the home has a vertical design. The eleven-foot windows are unusually tall. Manufactured in France, the twelve windows—complete with casings, facings, moldings, and blinds—were shipped to New Orleans, then loaded onto a steamer bound for Jefferson.

The simple rectangular floor plan has a central hall and four rooms. The roof, however, is framed as though the residence consisted of a central block with two end pavilions. The high-pitched roof has a dragon-cut tin ridge cap. Detailing on the gabled eves is typical of the French Victorian style.

Included in the National Registry of Historic Places, Historic Homes of Texas, and the Smith Guide to America, the French Townhouse received landmark status in 1965.

Bateman-Rowell

307 North Vale Street

The Bateman-Rowell house was built in 1862. Albert H. Rowell moved into the house in 1884. He was one of three brothers who migrated to Texas along with the Culberson family in the late 1860s. The Rowell brothers all found success in Jefferson. Albert became a deacon of the First Baptist Church. He was elected Jefferson's mayor in 1902 and held that position until 1907. His brother J. H. Rowell owned and operated tenement houses in Jefferson. The third brother, D. E. Rowell, was a prominent doctor in the town.

The home exudes a warm and welcoming feeling, while its classic style transcends time. It features a three-quarter porch, a popular Texas architectural style of its time. The house was the first in Jefferson to have a gas meter installed, probably due to Albert's prominence. The meter is still visible in the home today, under a small door in the floorboards. The lace curtains in the two front parlors are nearly 140 years old, and the floors are heart of pine. The house has six fireplaces, some featuring their original mantels.

The home is unique in Jefferson because all the original outbuildings are still on the property. The backyard holds a chicken coop, outhouse, washroom, and servants' quarters. Strolling the property, it's easy to imagine life in Jefferson in the 1800s and to reflect on how much easier life is today.

Sedberry-DeSpain

412 Market Street

An editor of a Confederate newspaper, a cotton merchant, an attorney, a dentist, a schoolteacher, a pharmacist, a steamboat owner, two drugstore owners, and a federal employee have all owned the Sedberry House. Records do not indicate who built it, but 1854 deed records from Marion County list W. F. Smith as owner of a house and Lots One, Two, and Three on Block 27 of the Urquhart Addition. Smith owned the house until 1867, when he sold it to Richard C. Boney.

The longest residents were Lelia and George Sedberry, and the home remained in their family for sixty-three years. Mr. Sedberry, a former captain in the Confederate army, was the founder of Sedberry Drug Store, known as the oldest drugstore in Texas. He was also owner of the steamer *Anna Tardy,* using a dock in Port Jefferson.

The home is a mix of architectural styles: a Louisiana-style raised cottage with distinct touches of Spanish influence.

It is said that the home was built as a replica of one in New Orleans. Its double wrought iron staircases dominate the entrance and set it apart as one of the distinctive houses in Jefferson. The brick basement and columns in the front complement the Greek Revival columns on the upper story. The second-floor columns have detailing and capitals, adding grandeur to the home.

The interior still has many original details, including a gas chandelier with plaster ceiling rosettes and faux-painted marble around the fireplace.

Beard-DeWare

212 Vale Street

The Beard House is particularly outstanding for its architecture. It is one of the finest residences in Jefferson, and was cited in 1936 by the United States Department of the Interior as possessing exceptional historic and architectural interest and being worthy of careful preservation. Architectural house plans are recorded in the Library of Congress.

The Beard House is located on property originally part of the Allen Urquhart Survey. The property changed hands several times before Noble A. Birge bought it in 1861 from William Perry, builder of the Excelsior Hotel. Deed records indicate that Birge, a prominent merchant and civic leader, built the house about 1860.

The architecture has two distinct entrances on Vale and Henderson streets. Much of the ornamental trim details on the home are reminiscent of grand salon interiors from the steamboats that docked at nearby Jefferson's busy wharf.

The home was recorded as a Texas Historic Landmark in 1966.

Hudgins-Blake

1010 Line Street

The home known as the Hudgins-Blake serves as a reminder of Jefferson's past. It was built by George Whitcorn in 1867, not far from sites that had played a role in the Civil War: the Yankee Stockade Prison Camp and training camps for the cavalry and infantry soldiers.

The house is near the river in the "Sand Town Hill" area. Many of Jefferson's early Jewish families called "The Hill" home.

The property changed hands several times before William and Mattie Blake purchased the home in 1897. The Blakes were prominent African American educators in Marion County. William was later the superintendent for Jefferson's "colored" schools. Blake family ownership continued until 1957. The home was passed down to their daughter Frances, a Marshall resident and teacher, who sold the property to the McDonalds. They restored the home in the early 1960s, and it received landmark status in 1973.

Like many of Jefferson's historic homes, the Hudgins-Blake has an exterior of the Greek Revival style, which emphasizes symmetry. The front porch, with its simple columns, conveys the feeling of classic Southern hospitality.

The home's Greek Revival facade hides the dog-trot style interior. Floor-to-ceiling windows and thirteen-foot ceilings add grandeur while also serving a practical purpose. The extra-tall windows opened from the floor up, reaching eight feet. When opened, they allowed the cool breeze to float in from the nearby river and improve air circulation during those long, hot, East Texas summer days.

The home's larger rooms and one bedroom are devoted to President Lincoln. The Lincoln Room features collectibles and wallpaper that replicates the wall covering in Ford's Theater where Lincoln was assassinated. The house is furnished with an eclectic mix of antiques.

Singleton–Virginia Cross

401 Soda Street

The Singleton home, built in 1859 by Buckner Abernathy, is in the older portion of town, close to the Jefferson Historic District. In 1885, Capt. W. E. Singleton purchased the home. He had served as an officer in the Confederate army during the Civil War. The Singleton family maintained ownership of the home for one hundred years. In 1926, Captain Singleton's granddaughter, Ellie Mae Singleton (Mrs. Bennie) Moseley, inherited the home and lived in it until 1985.

The home is an excellent example of early Texas Greek Revival architecture that was patterned after eighteenth-century Virginia houses of the cross plan, hence the sobriquet Virginia Cross. The front portico with a gabled pediment and second-floor balcony is the only one of its kind in Jefferson.

The house has a large central hallway with doors at the front and back that provided cross ventilation in early times. The front portion of the house is two-story, with a stair in the central hall. When viewed in plan, the projecting front porch, central hall, and front rooms make up a cruciform layout.

The Virginia Cross is constructed of cypress lumber, and the exterior walls are covered with cypress clapboards. All of the floors are original wide-plank heart pine. The parlor and central hall are decorated with period wallpaper.

This significant example of antebellum architecture is a recorded Texas Historic Landmark, is on the National Register of Historic Places, and is documented in the Historic American Building Survey in the Library of Congress.

Magnolias

209 Broadway

The Magnolias is one of the outstanding homes in Jefferson. Although built after the Civil War, it is strongly Greek Revival in character and an example of the continuing appeal of this style in Texas long after it fell out of fashion in the east. The attached colonnaded front gallery, the detail of the capitals, the window architraves, the wide entablature, and the handsome and unusual front door moldings are all continuations of the style.

Daniel Alley, an early Jefferson settler and donor of the land for the city, built the Magnolias. Alley and his wife lived in the home until 1873, when Mrs. Alley deeded the property to her daughter, Victoria Alley Crawford.

The Crawfords lived at the Magnolias for three years. After Victoria Crawford's death in 1876, her husband sold the house to Col. W. B. Ward, a native Texan who moved to Jefferson soon after the Civil War. He was one of the town's leading businessmen and president of the Jefferson National Bank when Jefferson was the largest river port in Texas.

He was also a promoter of the East Line Red River Railroad, a venture promoted by Jefferson citizens in 1871, when they saw their prominence as a river port being threatened by the building of railroads to Dallas, Shreveport, and Houston.

The Magnolias, named for the large trees that grow around the house, was more than a home for prominent Jefferson businessmen. It was also a civic and social center for many years and the oldest chartered club in Texas, the "1881 Club." It was organized in October 1881 as the oldest member and pioneer unit in the Texas State Federation of Women's Clubs.

602 Taylor Street

The Schulter home, on the corner of Taylor and South Line streets, was thought to be the tallest house in Jefferson at the time it was built. It had a widow's walk, a small railed platform at the roof level. The architectural feature was so named because this is where women were thought to watch ships dock while awaiting the safe return of their husbands and loved ones. The Schulter home was the only house in town with a widow's walk.

The land was purchased in 1847, and construction began in 1850. The three-story house, with large sheltered porches on both street entrances, was completed in 1856.

The home remained in the Schulter family until 1948, when Mr. and Mrs. Blains purchased it from a granddaughter of the original occupants.

Emmert-Dolan

408 Jefferson Street

In 1868, George B. Draper gave a deed of trust for $918 and lumber to G. W. Keene to build the Emmert-Dolan house. The home changed hands several times within a short period. In 1898, Alice Tucker, widow of J. M. Tucker and owner at the time, sold it to Alice Emmert.

The home was late Greek Revival style, with fourteen-foot ceilings, nine larger rooms, and three fireplaces (unusual at the time). Renovations in 1915 brought the bathrooms and kitchen into the house.

Alice Emmert never married and lived in the home for the rest of her life. In 1908, she was the first women elected to public office in Texas. She served as county school superintendent and maintained that position until she retired in 1920. Ms. Emmert was very influential in Marion County and was a member of the 1881 Social Club in Jefferson. In 1925-1926, Claudia Taylor (Lady Bird Johnson) attended school in Jefferson and was a boarder in Alice's home.

A later resident was Mrs. Dolan, a popular music teacher in Jefferson schools for two decades. She also played the organ at the First United Methodist Church and gave piano lessons in the home's front parlor.

The Emmert-Dolan house received a Texas Historic Marker in 1974.

Benefield

909 Line Street

The Benefield home was purchased by author Barry Benefield's parents in 1897. The family moved in when Barry was nineteen. He left soon after to attend the University of Texas before moving to Dallas to begin his career at the *Dallas Morning News*. However, Benefield soon left Texas to work for the *New York Times*. He went on to work in public relations for the Henry Holt publishing firm and marry a fellow Texan, Lucillia Stallcup, in 1913.

Later, Benefield began writing novels and screenplays. He would base stories around Jefferson, calling it "Crebillion, Louisiana." He retired from writing novels in 1947.

Benefield returned to Jefferson in 1960 after Lucillia's death and became known for his daily treks through the streets to visit the library. It was noted that he was the only person in Jefferson who checked out multiple books each day. Although often seen around town, he was described as standoffish toward the townspeople. He died in 1971 at the age of ninety-three.

The home was fully restored in 1980. The new owners used bricks and shutters from a New Orleans building known as "The Bank."

The Benefield home received a Texas Historical Commission marker in 1984.

Freeman Plantation

Highway 49 West

Williamson M. Freeman; his wife, Drucilla; and their three children lived in Talbot County, Georgia, before coming to Jefferson in the late 1840s. They moved their possessions on a wagon to New Orleans. The Freemans also brought their slaves from Georgia, walking alongside the wagon. At New Orleans, the group loaded everything onto a steamboat and rode up the Red River. Irma Grannana, a Freeman descendant, describes the Red River as the gateway to north Texas. Galveston was the largest port to the south and west Texas.

Williamson Freeman became a successful merchant in Jefferson. He also founded Jefferson Baptist Church. Freeman would travel to New York City twice a year to purchase goods. Then with *Alligator,* his steamboat, he delivered the goods around the Jefferson and Marshall area. Freeman built a warehouse on the Big Cypress and he dealt in dry goods, groceries, and European textiles.

The sugar and cotton plantation was established in 1850 on a tract of 1,100 acres. Deed records show another nine-acre tract was obtained with an old "house place." In 1997, archeologist Claude McCrocklin found evidence of earlier Anglo-Texans while excavating the property. McCrocklin found Indian arrowheads, as well as fragments of late eighteenth-century European china. The house, constructed by Freeman's slaves, is a typical Greek Revival raised cottage, in that the steps go to the second floor. The bricks were handmade on site.

The resident blacksmith, "Uncle George," is said to have created the ironwork in the house. An original door hinge remains in the lower level of the home.

The craftsmen used square nails in the home's construction. The house was built on a hill by the busy crossroads out of Jefferson. The original road heading toward Dallas is still visible today.

The Freemans loved their home but when Drucilla became ill and died, Williamson lost his will to live. He refused to eat, and he died a short time later. The children, whose interests were not in East Texas, inherited the home.

The house went through several owners until it was left vacant in the 1930s. Tenant farmers used the house for storage until 1937, when it was purchased by Lawrence and Augusta Flannery. They restored the structure and built a modern addition.

Lawrence Flannery was a flamboyant old tycoon who led a wild life. Because of his poker nights, iron bars were placed on the ground-floor windows. The Flannery parties were so large that sometimes the dancing overflowed into the central hall.

In the 1970s, the DeWare family purchased the home. Today it is a private residence. It remains true to its Greek Revival style with the white walls and green shutters. However, the iron bars remain to commemorate the home's wild time in the 1930s.

Falling Leaves

304 Jefferson Street

John Sabine built the Greek Revival home in 1855, originally naming it Magnolia Hill. The house contained four large rooms and one large central hall. Due to fire hazard, the kitchen was built as a detached structure (a common practice of that time).

In 1858, a widow, Mrs. Margaret Amoss, purchased the home. She had two daughters, Eloise and Sally Amoss. Eloise became the longest inhabitant of the home, residing there for more than sixty years.

In the late 1800s, the home was enlarged with the addition of an "ell" to the original four rooms and hallway.

Eloise Amoss Fosque Thomas sold the home to J. B. Whelan in 1920. In 1961, the home was purchased by Baltzar and Doris Koontz, who renamed the property Falling Leaves.

The home was sold in 1992 to Joe and Barbara Bell. After a ten-month restoration, the house opened its doors as Falling Leaves Bed and Breakfast Inn.

The property was sold again in July 2000 to Michael G. and Lisa Barry who continue to welcome overnight guests into their home.

The home received its Texas Historic Seal in 1965.

Mosley Manor

412 N. Soda Street

This Greek Revival home was originally a "dog trot" floor plan with an open breezeway. It was constructed of native cypress wood in 1851 by the first druggist to come to this part of Texas, Mr. J. C. Preston. The large handmade windows (original to the home) and twelve-foot ceilings helped cool the home in summer. Twin fireplaces on each side kept the winter chill away.

In 1863, during the "War of Northern Aggression," the home was sold to Judge Seaborn Moseley. Judge Moseley and his descendants owned the home for more than eighty years. After the last Moseley (Miss Mabel Moseley—a beloved piano teacher in Jefferson) moved away, the house became sadly derelict. At one time, a tree grew up through (and destroyed) one of the original fireplaces. However, the old home refused to give in to the ravages of neglect. For twenty years, it saw duty as a duplex home for two families. It was later known as Gone with the Wind restaurant. Still later, it served as a bed and breakfast inn.

Present owners, Joe and Vicki Lee, purchased the property in 1997. They have devoted much loving work and care to this Texas Historic Landmark home.

Homes from 1870-1890

Early Victorian structures were simple in style until after the Civil War when they became more complex. They were designed from the inside out. The layout of rooms and flow determined the outward look. The outside became decorative, elaborate and flamboyant using a variety of details.

Terry-McKinnon

109 Henderson Street

The T. S. Terry house was built by S. D. Rainey, a wealthy cotton merchant. He built the home in 1880, at the height of the Victorian period, when design was sometimes extravagant. Differing from the modest Greek Revival style, asymmetrical plans with a multitude of rooms and steeply pitched gable roofs were popular. During Reconstruction, understated architecture was not a concern for the newly wealthy.

The home was purchased by Mary M. Terry in 1886 and remained in the Terry family until 1994.

The two-story Victorian style home, with its modest gingerbread adornments, featured fourteen-foot ceilings and heart of pine floors. Eight of the rooms had fireplaces, two of which were coal burning with cast iron mantels.

As with many of the early homes, the kitchen and bath were originally detached from the main structure. After the kitchen was incorporated, the water well was part of the home, with a cistern in the backyard.

The McKinnon family has since purchased the home and performed extensive restorations.

Epperson – House of the Seasons

409 S. Alley

Built in 1872, during Jefferson's prosperous time, the Epperson home, known as the House of the Seasons, illustrates the people and life of the time. The home was built for Benjamin Holland Epperson and received its name for the colored glass in its Italian-style cupola.

Epperson was born in Amite County, Mississippi, and moved to Texas in 1846. He attended Princeton Law School before moving to Texas. While he did not graduate, the Texas bar admitted him to practice law in 1847. Epperson became a prominent political figure in Texas and lived in Clarksville. He was a friend of Sam Houston and a fixture in the Texas legislature for numerous sessions. He represented the Cherokee Indians in their claims against the Bureau of Indian Affairs. He ran unsuccessfully for governor as a member of the Whig party in 1851. In 1870, Epperson married Amanda Shields and moved to Jefferson. Their marriage produced five children. After settling in Jefferson, Epperson purchased land from James Rodgers in 1871. Home construction began for the growing family. The likely architect was Arthur Gilman, a notable New York City and Boston architect. The home at its core is a classic Greek Revival, but the Victorian-era details illustrate the transition between classic elegance and the heavy detail trend that began in the late 1800s. Corinthian columns and the cupola make the home unique. Italianate features include the arched and slender windows, the bay windows, and the bracketed cornices.

The home's cupola adds to its uniqueness with the colored glass depicting the seasons. The blue glass on the north side creates a chilly feeling in the person who peers out the window. The red and orange glass on the east and western sides create the feeling of summer and fall. Lastly, the south windows feature green glass to instill the feeling of spring. While the glass provides an artistic flair, it is said it aided in warming the bath water in the home. Inside the structure are other artistic elements that add

character to the dwelling. An Italian-style mural is painted in the home's dome. The mural is visible from a well-like opening in the first story. Vertical grain pine floors and Italian marble fireplaces add to the opulence. Referred to as a "complete plantation," the

home had outbuildings for chickens, kitchen, laundry, and a lumber house. The original buildings are no longer there, but the home is left as a marvel of the late 1800s architecture.

After completion, the Epperson's enjoyed their new home, but sadly, Amanda died in 1872. Epperson remarried in 1874 to Nancy Blinn of Clarksville. They had two children of their own. The home had some adjustments made sometime after completion when Epperson's children upset their stepmother by sneaking out via the rear staircase. It is said that she swore she'd have the stairs removed if they continued to misbehave.

Apparently, she was true to her word because the staircase is no longer there.

Unfortunately, Mr. Epperson had only six short years to enjoy his mansion. He died of typhoid fever in 1878. Many people attended his funeral. Mourners came from as far away as Marshall (a twenty-minute drive now but a full day's travel during horse-and-buggy time).

After Epperson's death, the home went to his wife but was sold out of the family in 1906 when Marion Glass, a local grocer, purchased the home for himself and his wife. After her

death in 1925, Glass opened a boarding house. He most likely needed companionship and the large home and visitors filled that need. After Glass's death, the home was sold to Dr. W. S. McNutt for $2,500.

Dr. McNutt chartered Four States University on the site. Classes were held in two front parlors and on the front porch. The college ran for several years. Dr. McNutt owned the home until his death in 1971. Then the home became a private residence again. The home received its historical landmark in 1965, as one of the earliest and most beautiful acknowledged landmarks in the city.

Wise Manor

312 Houston Street

Wise Manor is a registered Texas Historic Landmark. The charming pre-Civil War cottage is filled with family heirlooms, Victorian antiques and Jefferson history. The house stands on the corner of Houston and Camp streets, just above the place where the ferry brought adventure, commerce, and provisions to early Jefferson.

Owner Susan Wise maintains her home and bed-and-breakfast business as a tribute to her mother, Katherine Ramsay Wise, who was Jefferson's longtime town historian.

Nearby is the site of the Union stockade, where Southern prisoners awaited trial during Reconstruction. General Buell, commandant of the occupying Union forces, made himself a guest at Wise Manor until he commandeered the house that once stood across the street.

Jacob and Ernestine Sterne once lived in the home, and Mrs. Sterne succeeded her husband as Jefferson's postmaster after the Civil War. The Sternes were leading members of what was once a large Jewish population in Jefferson. Their children memorialized the family by commissioning a fountain that now stands at the intersection of Lafayette and Market streets.

Evergreen House

405 Delta. Evergreen House was built in 1889 and remained in the same family for seventy years. The current owners have beautifully restored it.

Pride House

409 Broadway. Pride House began as a boarding house during the oil boom of the 1930s. Later, in 1979, it became the first bed and breakfast to open in Texas.

J. H. Benefield~Gay 90s

1009 Line Street

The J. H. Benefield House, also known as the Gay 90s house, is a good example of Queen Anne Victorian style. The original owner of the site was Daniel N. Alley, who owned the land and sold lots for $500 in gold coins. J. P. Harvey and his wife purchased the lot for the home.

The house was built in 1890 by E. S. Hooper and Will Singleton, co-owners of a sawmill on the Big Cypress Bayou;

they constructed several fine homes in Jefferson.

The original structure was recorded as a one-story frame house with six rooms, a porch, and one bathroom.

In 1907, J. H. Benefield, a bachelor and brother of the famous novelist Barry Benefield, purchased the house for $2,000. He eventually married Justa Glass, and they raised two children in the home.

Victorian Castle

301 Clarksville

The Victorian Castle was built in the 1890s by William E. Singleton Jr. for his wife, Victoria. The home is named both for her and for its architectural style.

The Singletons had six children, all of whom were said to be musically inclined. The family entertained in the parlor, where the original piano still resides. Several of the children lived on the same street after marrying.

Additional Historic Homes

Guarding Oak, 301 S. Friou

Rowell, 207 Alley

Oak Alley, 900 Line Street

Grove, 405 E. Moseley

Succession, 310 E. Jefferson

McKay, 306 E. Delta

Clark, 201 Henderson

Homestead, 410 Delta

Interiors

Many interiors were done in the grand manner reflecting well on their owners and builders. The notable increase in prosperity that accompanied the Industrial Revolution created a new middle class. Home interiors were used to show off newfound cultural interest, prosperity, and status. Typical of a middle-class drawing room was an abundance of furniture, fabrics, and decoration.

Most of the Greek Revival homes were designed with an emphasis on scale and proportions. The plan was traditionally symmetrical, with rooms of similar scale on either side of the large central hall. The hall was important as a receiving room and living space, as well as for providing through ventilation.

Central Hallways

Virginia Cross

Freeman Plantation

Cavalier

Sedberry, parlor

Boudoirs

Beard-DeWare

Freeman Plantation

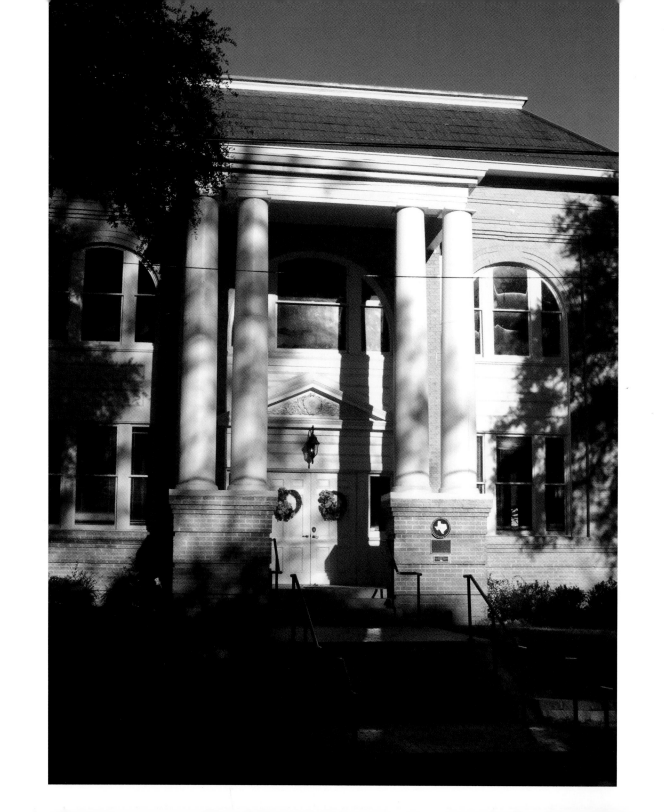

Buildings

Jefferson Carnegie Library

301 W. Lafayette Street

The Carnegie Library of Jefferson, Texas, celebrated one hundred years of service to the residents of Marion County in November 2007, after undergoing a spectacular renovation. It was one of thirty-four Carnegie funded libraries in Texas. Only four of the original structures are still used as libraries.

The library of Jefferson formally began in 1903 with a handful of books. In 1907, the Andrew Carnegie Foundation of Pittsburgh, Pennsylvania, endowed the library with two grants, stipulating that the city of Jefferson provide the land and its upkeep. From 1886 until 1919, Carnegie donated more than $40 million, which paid for almost 1,700 new libraries across America. J. F. Berry of Morris County was chosen as the Jefferson building contractor, with a bid of $8,750.

When the library opened its doors, funds were raised with $0.10 teas and $1 annual membership drives. Over the years, the building has been in continuous use as a library. In addition, the upstairs has been used as a school, dance studio, Red Cross Center, office space for various government agencies, museum, and sewing center for the needy.

In 1961, the city of Jefferson transferred title to the Jefferson Library Association, forming a nonprofit organization.

Prior to 1991, most of the library's books were used or donated. The entire collection has been updated and expanded to encourage literacy and the use of technology in the pursuit of lifelong learning. The physical building has been meticulously restored to its historic glory.

Artificial gas retort

Haywood House

202 Market Street

Constructed in 1865, the Haywood House Hotel was advertised as the finest hotel west of the Mississippi. At the time, it was the largest building in the Port of Jefferson, Texas. The original structure, built by Georgia-born H. P. Mabry, was four stories high and extended the full length of Market Street from Dallas Street to Lake Street. It was located on Big Cypress Bayou just above the port in the commercial district.

The hotel had one of the first elevators in town.

A tunnel under the hotel ran to the river, and stories circulated through the years that this tunnel was used to hide fugitives and runaway slaves who needed to catch a steamboat under the dark of night. The tunnel was uncovered during renovations in 2003.

Mabry, his wife, Abbie Haywood Mabry, and their children were joined in residence at the hotel by her parents and other family members. Also living there was W. G. Rives, who assisted in the operation of the hotel, along with his wife and daughter.

Among the first regular residents of the Haywood House were federal army officers who commanded the occupying forces encamped in the freewheeling river port of Jefferson. Board and lodging was advertised as $10 per month, payable weekly, with board alone $7.50 per month.

The fire of 1871 reduced the grand hotel to a quarter of its original size. The remaining structure was restored as a family residence for the Haywood-Mabry family and furnished with fine antiques; it remained a family residence until 1962.

Clarence C. Braden, a locally known philanthropist, was the last descendent of the Haywood-Mabry family to reside in the Haywood House. After his death in 1962, a fortune in coins was found in the building. A two-ton truck used to carry Braden's massive savings to the bank reportedly could only be driven in low gear because of the tremendous weight of the cigar boxes, churns, and suitcases that held his cache of coins. This event made international news, with reporters converging on Jefferson to cover the story.

The Haywood House then lay in ruins for almost twenty years, gutted by the search for treasure. Gary Hurst of Dallas purchased Haywood House in the late 1980s and restored the building for commercial use. The building housed retail establishments and a dinner theater for several years.

The Haywood House was purchased in the early 1990s by a Texas nonprofit corporation headed by B. B. Barr and Johnny Roe of Dallas to become the home of the Texas History Museum, housing a collection of rare Texana and banking artifacts.

Paul and Carol Harrell purchased Haywood House in June 2005 as their private residence.

Jefferson Hotel

124 W. Austin Street

Built in 1851, the Jefferson Hotel, at 124 W. Austin Street, began as a cotton warehouse along the busy banks of the Cypress River. When the steamboat traffic came to a stop in the 1870s, it became a stylish hotel that has changed owners and names several times over the years.

61 Dallas Street

The red brick building in the early commercial district of Jefferson was built in 1860 by John B. Ligon, a contractor and wagon merchant. The building started as a livery, but in 1863, it housed a Confederate hat factory operated by Kate G. Sutton. By 1864, it was McGarity's Saloon and continued to flourish as such until 1868. During the Reconstruction era, it was a warehouse owned by Ephrium C. Terry, a local cotton merchant and owner of several properties along Dallas Street.

There were several fires in the commercial district from 1868 to 1877. At least one blaze reached 61 Dallas Street, partially burning the structure. William H. Mason, a Jefferson lawyer and Confederate veteran, purchased the building and restored it to its current appearance.

As Jefferson's economy declined and the bayou receded, the building was used by various lodge organizations as a meeting hall. The Jefferson Masonic Lodge renovated the structure in 1916 and occupied the building until 1950.

It is one of the few remaining structures from the Jefferson steamboat wharf district along Dallas Street. Under the guidance of David Robertson, the Jefferson Junior Historians spent more than 6,000 student work hours restoring the building in 1971. They received numerous awards, including the National Trust for Historic Preservation Award, which was presented in Washington. In 1976, the building became the first "historic laboratory" for high-school studies of Texas history. It served as the home theater for Jefferson Junior Historians musical performances for twenty-nine years.

The building was purchased in 2003 as a private residence. It has been restored as a historic saloon and townhouse.

Excelsior Hotel

211 W. Austin Street

The Excelsior Hotel graces the center of town on Austin Street and is central to the town's activities and to the history of Jefferson.

The hotel began as a residence for Capt. William Perry and his family. He was the owner of dredge boats and awarded the first contract to open navigation through Caddo Lake and beyond, bringing the first steamboat to Jefferson. The north portion of the Excelsior was built in a Classic Revival two-story style in 1858. He opened the upstairs rooms for rent and called it the Irvin House. After Perry's sudden death, due to mistaken identity, in front of the hotel in 1869, the hotel had several names and owners. It was called the Commercial Hotel, Exchange, and finally in 1877, Mrs. Kate Wood acquired it under the name the Excelsior.

During the 1870s, Jefferson was a thriving town. There were lots of people coming and going with commercial activity. Mrs. Wood quickly noticed the influx of people and built a wing to the hotel to accommodate the "drummers," traveling salesmen. The rooms were tiny, just big enough for a dresser and chair. There was a fireplace and window in each room. Every room had a bowl and pitcher, and in the corner of the courtyard was a cistern that caught the rainwater off the roof. Out houses were still located in the back courtyard.

She ran the establishment until 1907 and passed it to her daughter, Amelia McNeely, and in 1920, Amelia bequeathed it to George Niedermeier (her faithful employee). The hotel has remained in continuous operation since it opened, which makes it one of the oldest establishments of its kind still in operation. It underwent major renovation in 1954 and was acquired in 1962 by the Jessie Allen Wise Garden Club. To this day, it is still owned and operated by the club as a museum and hotel.

During Jefferson's heyday many famous people stayed at the hotel. Among them were two presidents, Ulysses S. Grant and Rutherford B. Hayes; financiers John Jacob Astor, Jay Gould, and W. E. Vanderbilt; and playwright Oscar Wilde.

An 1871 advertisement for the Excelsior declared, "Stages arrive and depart from this hotel daily." Even though the modes of transportation have changed, the historic hotel remains to accommodate travelers with the Southern hospitality of a more leisurely time.

Jefferson Historical Museum

223 W. Austin Street

The building on the corner of Austin and Market in the heart of downtown Jefferson was originally a federal courthouse and post office. Construction began in 1888 and took eighteen months, at a cost of $6,000.

On the first floor was the post office and inspector's station. The second floor held the courtroom and judge's quarters, U.S. marshal's office, and court clerk's office. The jury room was on the third floor.

Today the building is home to the Jefferson Historical Museum, which is operated by the Jefferson Historical Society. The society and museum were established in 1948 to preserve the town's history and artifacts. Many treasures and belongings have been donated and collected from families who have lived in the Jefferson area.

Jefferson Churches

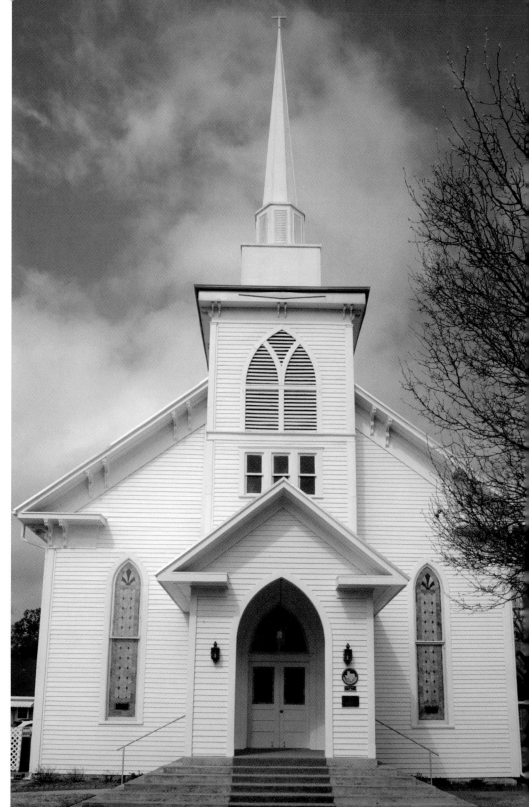

First United Methodist Church,
305 W. Henderson

The influences of church congregations became evident in Jefferson during the 1850s. However, the First United Methodist Church was formed earlier, in 1844, when the East Texas Conference appointed James Baldridge as minister to the Methodist Episcopal Church. By 1848, it had grown from fifty-three members to a sufficient size to support a full-time pastor. Allen Urquhart sold the Methodist trustees a lot for $100 to build a brick church and parsonage to accommodate the enlarged congregation. To grace the new steeple, extending sixty feet above the roof crest, a bell pealed. A. F. Schluter was known to have donated 1,500 Mexican silver coins to add to the making of the bell, thus giving it a silver tone. It can still be heard today.

The Cumberland Presbyterian Church was organized between 1846 and 1850. In 1872, on the corner of Line and Jefferson Street north of the city park, work began on an intricate brick design building with a towering spire top. Built by John Ligon, the sanctuary became the largest in town. The church steeple had an unusual feature; where mechanical clocks would normally be installed, clock faces had been painted on the four sides of the base of the steeple. It is believed the clocks were painted as a reminder of the starting times of services. When the steeple was repaired in 1981, the panels disappeared.

The organization of the Jefferson Baptist church began in March 1855. Williamson Freeman, a new resident from Georgia, became a successful wholesale mercantile business owner and a devout Baptist and joined several other town residents, including his wife and children, to form the First Baptist Church of Jefferson. Without a meetinghouse of their own, the small congregation met at the Union House in the city park, Judge Patillo's schoolhouse, and other churches until they were large enough to construct a church. A brick building was completed in 1864 under the leadership of C. S. McCloud, their pastor at the time. The church had a large upper balcony reserved for slaves who attended services with their masters. The black community later moved and built Union Mission Baptist Church. The First Baptist Church of Jefferson hosted the first meeting of the Southern Baptist Convention to be held west of the Mississippi on May 7, 1874. The early building on Polk Street was destroyed in flames and a new one was erected in 1944.

On June 8, 1860, Bishop Alex Gregg organized an Episcopal church and a building was constructed on Main Street on the west side of the city park.

Lots were donated by James M. Murphy and Allen Urquhart on the corner of Polk and Lafayette streets to Claudius M. Debuis of Galveston to help begin the building of a Roman Catholic church. The Immaculate Conception Catholic Church now stands at the corner of Vale and Lafayette streets and is the oldest parish in the Dallas diocese.

What is now Jefferson Playhouse, owned and restored by the Jessie Allen Wise Garden Club in 1965, was once a Catholic girls school and Jewish synagogue. The Historical Marker states, "Built about 1860 by Robert W. Nesmith, a contractor of stage lines. After several changes in ownership, the house was purchased in 1869 for the Sisters of Charity and used as their convent, hospital and school (called St. Mary's). In 1875, property was bought by Sinai Hebrew Congregation of Jefferson. An auditorium was added, and served as the local synagogue until about 1900."

Cumberland Presbyterian Church

First Baptist Church of Jefferson

Christ Episcopal Church

Jefferson Playhouse (front view)

Immaculate Conception Catholic Church

Jefferson Playhouse (back view)

Landmarks

Gould Car

"Atalanta," 201 W. Austin Street

The Jay Gould rail car was built in 1888, by the American Car & Foundry Business of St. Charles, Missouri. It was used as Mr. Gould's personal railroad car for business travels. A native of New York, Gould was a noted financier and the owner of numerous railroad companies, including the Union Pacific, the Missouri Pacific, the International & Great Northern, and the Texas Pacific. This car, named Atalanta, remained in Gould family ownership until the 1930s. Elaborately designed and elegantly furnished, the Atalanta features two observation rooms, four staterooms, two baths, a butler's pantry, kitchen, dining room, and office. Interior materials include mahogany and curly maple woodwork, silver bathroom accessories, and crystal light fixtures. Following Jay Gould's death in 1892, the car was used by his son, George Jay Gould (president of the Texas and Pacific Railroad), and his wife, actress Edith Kingston. The car later was brought to Texas from St. Louis and used as a family residence during the 1930s East Texas oil boom. Purchased in 1953 by the Jessie Allen Wise Garden Club, it was moved to its current site in 1954.

Jay Gould was known as a railroad developer and held a reputation as a robber baron of railroad stocks. At the time, he was considered to be one of the wealthiest men in America. By 1880, he was in control of 10,000 miles of railway in the United States. According to one legend, Gould came to Jefferson wanting right of way for the transcontinental line. However, Jeffersonians were confident in the steamboat trade. Their refusal to Mr. Gould caused him to cast a curse, declaring, "Grass would grow in the streets of Jefferson and the buildings house only bats." Jefferson continues to thrive as a small town and Jay Gould lives on as the town villain.

Sterne Fountain

Intersection of Market and Lafayette streets

The children of Jacob and Ernestine Sterne donated this statue in memory of their parents. It adorns the top of the splendid Sterne Fountain.

The Texas Historical Marker on the south corner of the intersection of Lafayette and Market streets describes the fountain as follows:

"Settling in Jefferson prior to the Civil War, Jacob and Ernestine Sterne became prominent leaders of the community. Their early management of the post office and their involvement in civic and cultural activities reflected the dramatic influence Jewish families had on the development of Jefferson."

In 1913, the Sternes' children gave the fountain to the city. Designed for use by people and animals, the fountain offers different drinking levels for dogs, horses, and humans.

The work was created by Guiseppe Moretti and cast by J. L. Mott Foundry of New York. The statue depicts Hebe, the Greek goddess of youth.

The Jefferson Mardi Gras Association later chose Hebe as the namesake for the organization.

Street view of the main street

Gas Stations

The First Texaco station on the main highway through Jefferson, Highway 49 at its intersection at Polk Street.

The 1920s Magnolia Oil gas station is now a restored bayou guesthouse, at intersection of Polk and Clarksville.

General Store

The General Store has been in operation as a hardware store, soda fountain, and drug store since the 1870s.

113 E. Austin

Afterword

Many thanks!

I could not have done this project without the help of friends sharing their time and talent: Eve Becker-Doyle, project consultant and editing; Rachel Garay-Kobb, design and layout; Linda Swift and Joe Lee, editing; Traci Hudson, intern from East Texas Baptist University, Marshall, Texas, research; and Jacques Jaubert and Lisa Hickok, hospitality and encouragement.

A grateful heart of appreciation goes out to the many individuals and friends who encouraged and supported me on this four-year journey of creating a visual documentary of the small East Texas town of Jefferson. Along the way, I have made new friends and discovered how a depth of history can spring from the most unassuming places.

I hope that my efforts will not only help share a glimmer of a time past, but also alert other small towns to the importance of protecting their architectural past and celebrating the history that goes with it.

After Jefferson's sudden decline in the late 1800s, it dropped from a boom-era population of 7,297 to nearly 3,000 and almost fell into a ghost town. However, core families and businesses continued to live and grow, and since the 1970s, people have moved back to Jefferson, restoring the older homes and enjoying an easier life of a time past. It now stands at a resurging population of 2,027.

Jay Gould's legendary curse of "grass will grow in your streets" has proved untrue more than one hundred years later.

References

Bolton, Theodore. "Historic Buildings of Marion County." http:// afrotexan.com/mar_build/index1.htm.

Bracken, Dorothy K., and Maurine W. Redway. *Early Texas Homes*. Dallas: Southern Methodist University Press, 1975.

Bagur, Jacques. *History of Navigation on Big Cypress Bayou and Lakes*. Denton, TX: University of North Texas Press, 2001.

Dean, Winnie Mathis. *Jefferson Queen of the Cypress*. Dallas: Van Nort and Company, 1955.

Echols, Gordon. *Early Texas Architecture*. Fort Worth, TX: Texas Christian University Press, 2000.

Historic American Buildings Survey, Heritage Documentation Programs, National Park Service. http://www.nps.gov/history/ hdp/habs/index.htm

Jeffersonian Newspaper published by Historic Jefferson Foundation, Jefferson, Texas.

McKenzie, Fred. *Avinger Texas, USA*. San Antonio: Watercress Press, 2003.

Tarpley, Fred. *Jefferson: Riverport to the Southwest*. Wolfe City, TX: Henington Publishing Company, 1983.

Texas Historical Commision Web site. Historic Sites Atlas for National Register Markers. http://atlas.thc.state.tx.us/.

———. "Texas Historic Seals of Homes in Marion County." http://www.thc.state.tx.us

Wise, Katherine. Historic research papers of Jefferson families and homes, Carnegie Library, Jefferson, Texas.

Other Sources

Oral history from homeowners:

De Spain, Sammie, president of Marion County Historical Commission

DeWare, Duke

Harvey, Mary Margaret Wise

Hudson, Traci, intern at East Texas Baptist University, Marshall, Texas

McKenzie, Fred

Omer, Laura

Parker, Vic, *Jefferson Jimplecute*, Jefferson, Texas

Wise, Susan

Records

Amon Carter Museum archives, Fort Worth, Texas

Jefferson Historical Museum Archives

Marion County Courthouse deed records